NODDING DOGS

&

VINYL ROOFS

First published in September 2007

A catalogue record for this book is available from the British Library

ISBN 978 1 84425 422 4

Library of Congress catalog card no 2007931167

Published by Haynes Publishing,
Sparkford, Yeovil, Somerset BA22 7JJ, UK
Tel: 01963 442030 Fax: 01963 440001
Int. tel: +44 1963 442030
Int. fax: +44 1963 440001
E-mail: sales@haynes.co.uk
Website: www.haynes.co.uk

Haynes North America Inc, 861 Lawrence Drive,
Newbury Park, California 91320, USA.

Printed and bound in Britain by
J. H. Haynes & Co. Ltd, Sparkford

PHOTO CREDITS

Motoring Picture Library, National Motor Museum, Beaulieu: 10, 12, 18, 19, 21, 33, 34, 36, 37, 40, 41, 43, 44, 46, 48, 51, 52, 53, 54, 57, 59, 60, 61, 62, 53, 64, 65, 71, 72, 73, 78, 81, 84, 85, 89, 93, 94, 95, 103, 104, 107, 108, 111, 115, 116, 117, 120
Breitling for Bentley: 20
Alfred Dunhill Ltd: 8, 13, 14, 15, 17, 23, 32, 47, 56, 67, 75, 83, 86, 87, 90, 92, 100, 105, 118
Jeff Colmer: 31
Jeni Panhorst: 112
Justin Wheeler: 31
Simon Reeves: 109
www.atrd.co.uk: 16
www.au-my.com: 38
www.autoanything.com: 27, 91, 101

www.autotrucktoys.com: 24
www.boysstuff.co.uk: 49
www.bumperdumper.com: 25
www.churchill.co.uk: 77
www.consolevault.com: 55
www.doggles.com: 35
www.flamekitz.com: 45
www.healiohealth.com: 79
www.kitsch.co.uk: 50, 80, 96
www.lightinsight.com: 67
www.maplin.co.uk: 39
www.phantomplate.com: 82
www.teamspirit.uk.com: 22
www.visiononwheels.com: 9

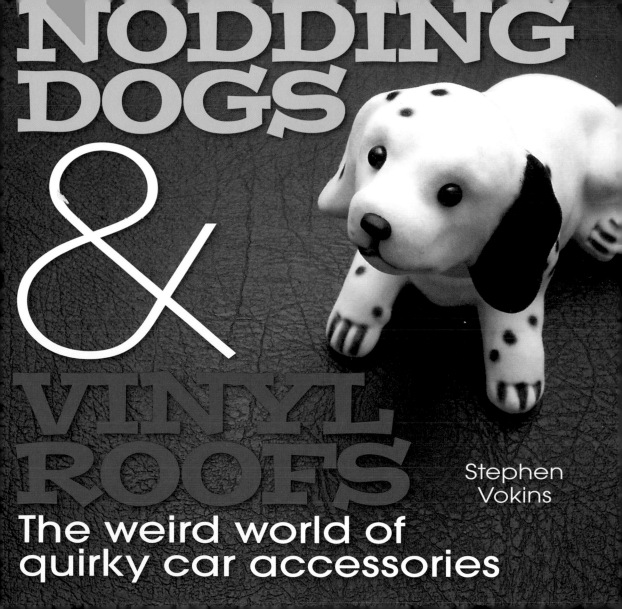

NODDING DOGS

&

VINYL ROOFS

Stephen
Vokins

The weird world of
quirky car accessories

CONTENTS

Dedication

This book is dedicated to my wonderful family, Mandy, Emma and Harry, and to the guys at Air1.com, whose great music accompanied the writing of this book.

With special thanks to:

Jon Pressnell, Mark Hughes, Derek Smith, John Lakey, Stephen Crawley, Jonathan Day, Andy Saunders, Tom Malcolm, Malquito Espina, Jeff Colmer, Simon Reeves, Jeni Panhorst, Tom Duengel, Justin Wheeler, Rebecca Hendrie, Andrea Wisden, Jason Boshoff,
Robert Fess – Auto Anything, Kelly Day,
Rob Halloway, Maria Lopez,
Flamekitz.com, Victoria Osborne,
Julia Marozzi, Kitsch.co.uk, Harj Banwait,
Frances Browning, Charlotte Moore,
Timothy Jackson, Anna Reynolds,
Bas de Jong, Jo Misson,
Brian Carpenter, Peter Tilley

INTRODUCTION

Owning a car can be an expensive business. Apart from the obvious expense of purchasing it in the first place, there's the fuelling, servicing, insuring and taxing of it to consider as well. And all that, before you start to personalise it.

Cars are so much more than transport: they are a canvas on which owners can demonstrate their streak of individuality. For some, the simple addition of stick-on trapped fingers to the lower edge of the boot-lid is sufficient to demonstrate a sense of humour and make the car that bit more personalised, whilst at the other extreme, should you wish to turn your exhaust pipe into a flame-thrower, the FlameKitz Exhaust Flame-Thrower Kit is the gadget for you. A common theme in the personalisation of cars has long been the endowment of a more sporty appearance, whether it be by painting the bonnet matt black or adding go-faster stripes.

The following pages show the breadth of car accessories that either is, or has been available to motorists keen to be different, or to improve their car in one way or another. The diversity of gadgets, trinkets and fripperies is almost beyond belief, and contributes to a huge, world-wide market in car accessories that plays an important role in the economies of many countries.

So read on, and chuckle at the ingenuity of some of the contents, marvel at the pointlessness of others, and see how many may have some appeal in the customisation of your car.

ACETYLENE LAMPS

In the days before electric lights, driving at night was even more perilous than by daylight. Candle lamps and oil-fired lamps were of more use for being seen than for seeing with, and once away from the gas-lit streets of the towns, a motorist was in very real danger of losing his way and meeting with all kinds of mishap.

Acetylene lamps provided a brighter light, though this was purely relative. They produced acetylene gas by the dripping of water (other naturally sourced fluids were found to work in cases of emergency) onto powdered calcium carbide, and the rate at which the water was allowed to drip regulated the amount of gas produced, thus the intensity of the flame. They were messy, however, and when electric lamps superseded them, few mourned their passing.

DUNHILL'S MOTORITIES

DISSOLVED ACETYLENE

EXHAUSTIVE experiments have conclusively proved to the satisfaction of the Home Office Authorities that Dissolved Acetylene is absolutely devoid of the smallest element of danger.

ALFRED DUNHILL, Ltd., have acquired from the patentees the sole right in Great Britain for the supply of Dissolved Acetylene in a form suitable for lighting motor cars and similar vehicles.

The following are some of the advantages secured by the Dissolved Acetylene system of lighting :—

The gas is delivered at the burners cool, dry, and at a steady pressure most suitable to ensure proper combustion and consequently maximum efficiency.

Can be turned on and lighted immediately.

Can be instantaneously extinguished without waste of gas.

Will not freeze. Will not choke the burners even when turned low.

Has no element of danger. There is no disagreeable smell.

Is easily manipulated. Will not corrode or choke the service pipe.

Does away with all unpleasant manipulations.

The consumption of the gas is shown by the gauge, so that the quantity remaining in the cylinder is known at a glance.

Increased brilliancy of the light due to pure gas, consequently permitting of small burners being used.

DISSOLVED ACETYLENE CONTAINER AND CASE.

Descriptive pamphlet giving full details of the system will be sent on application.

184

ADVERTISING HUBCAPS

The 21st-century world is a bewildering place, with advertisements seemingly everywhere. Each day we are subjected to huge numbers of marketing messages, and yet, it would appear, there is room for still more.

Vision on Wheels, a Dutch firm, sells throughout Europe hubcaps whose centres remain static whilst the car is moving, in much the same way (although with considerably less class) that the hubcap centres on the Rolls-Royce Phantom will always display the RR logo, regardless of the vehicle's speed.

The advertising hubcaps without doubt attract attention, which will please the advertiser, but do nothing to improve the appearance of the vehicle they adorn, the environment through which it drives, or road safety in general.

AIRMASTER DUST & INSECT DEFLECTOR

Originally popularised by the rally drivers of the day, the K-L Airmaster Dust & Insect Deflector was a small piece of transparent Perspex that was mounted at the front edge of the bonnet, often on the car's bonnet mascot.

The logic behind it was obvious: it aimed to alter the aerodynamics of the car's front and lift the incoming insects and other detritus clear of the windscreen. The reality, however, was that in most cases the car would need to be travelling at such a speed (and in the 1950s, when the Airmaster was popular, this would mostly have been at speeds higher than the average family car was capable of reaching), that it proved almost completely ineffective.

Interestingly, owners of the current Rolls-Royce Phantom are reputed to enjoy similar benefits derived from the huge frontal area of their impressive cars, which creates a bow-wave of pressure that blows over the top of the windscreen, thus keeping their screen clean, and passing the suicidal insects on to the car behind.

ALCO KEY

Saab is a company with a proud heritage of innovative thinking, and one of the more recent examples of this was the launch of trials in 2005 of the Alco Key in their native Sweden.

Aimed at eliminating the problem of drink-drivers, the Alco Key is fitted with a breathalyser, and users must first breathe into a small mouthpiece in the car's key fob before trying to start the car. A transponder in the key then communicates with the car's electronic control unit, immobilising the engine if a driver's breath sample is found to contain alcohol above the permitted level.

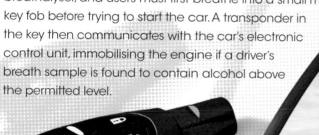

ANTI-DAZZLE MIRROR CLOCK

Combining three features in one gadget is a sure way of giving added appeal, and the Smiths Anti-Dazzle Mirror Clock was a popular accessory widely available in the 1930s in the UK.

Both stylish and useful, this little gadget would allow the driver to clock-watch and keep an eye on the traffic at the same time, although obviously there would be a certain blind-spot at the centre of the mirror, and its tint was designed to reduce the glare of increasingly brighter headlamps.

One flaw, however, could result from a late-running driver who may have felt less inclined to check his mirror regularly if each time he did so it reminded him of his poor timekeeping, thus causing him to be less aware of the cars behind him than might perhaps be desirable.

AUTO PUMP

Here's a great idea if you had a puncture in the front wheel of your Edwardian car. Once the puncture had been repaired and the tyre put back on the wheel, the chauffeur could be saved the final physical struggle of having to inflate manually the huge tyre if the owner had had the foresight to buy and fit the Auto Pump.

No-one can surely deny the ingenuity of such a contraption, assuming it worked properly, although the effort of jacking up the back wheel and fixing the pump in place must surely have offset most of the labour-saving advantages it offered.

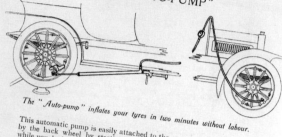

DUNHILL'S MOTORITIES

THE "AUTO-PUMP"

The "Auto-pump" inflates your tyres in two minutes without labour.

This automatic pump is easily attached to the car, and operated by the back wheel by starting the engine, inflates the tyres while you look on. It is always ready, and instantly detached when not in use, the only ... dy, and instantly detached under the footboard, ... eing two small brackets Well finished in ... and absolutely effective.
£2 15 0

YOUR TYRES INFLATED WITHOUT LABOUR IN 2 MINUTES.

STAND 197 (in the Gallery) **AT OLYMPIA.**

"The New Auto-Pump."

Detached when not in use. Two small brackets underneath footboard are the only fixtures. Subsequent adjustment simple.

Absolutely effective. Easily fixed. FULL PARTICULARS OF THE NEW PUMP ON APPLICATION.

THE DUNHILL "CARBOTRON" GARAGE STOVE.

RECOMMENDED BY INSURANCE COMPANIES.

PERFECTLY SAFE. NO SMELL.

NO FLUE REQUIRED. NO SMOKE.
21 -

21 -

Full particulars of stove and general catalogue sent on application.

DUNHILL'S

LONDON: 359-361, Euston Road, N.W. 2, Conduit Street, W.

Glasgow: 72, St. Vincent Street.

Manchester: 88, Cross Street.

THE BELSIZE HOOD

Early motorists had many trials to overcome, and apart from dressing for protection from the elements in the winter and clouds of dust in summer, coping with ridicule must surely have been one to overcome regularly.

Clothing such as the Belsize Hood, as sold in catalogues like Dunhill's Motorities were necessary for enduring the hardships of early motoring, yet despite the obvious efforts to make it seem a thing of beauty and luxury, such a garment can have done little to further the spread of the cause of motoring.

BELT FACE SHIELD

Necessity, as we all know, is the mother of invention, and desperation the mother of mistakes. This Edwardian attempt at providing the delicate female traveller with a degree of comfort has all the hallmarks of being an invention dreamt up in just such conditions.

Whilst modern open-top cars are reasonably draft-free, early cars were most definitely not, and travelling at any sort of pace would draw deep on one's reserves of stoicism. This screen was presumably invented in an attempt to convince the wives of motorcar owners that cars had a future, although keeping the damned thing off one's face and in a useful position as the car's pace increased must have been a full-time and enormously frustrating job.

BIOMETRIC IMMOBILISER

In recent years, cars have become more and more difficult for the amateur thief to drive away in. The days of breaking the steering lock and 'hot-wiring' the car have all but gone now, and with the Biometric Immobiliser, such a felonious enterprise would appear to be facing extinction.

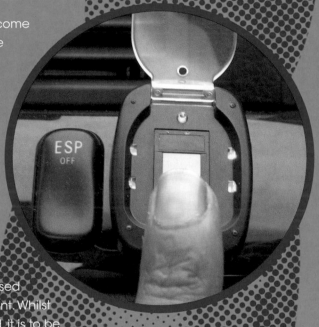

A car so fitted will start only after the correct key has been inserted and the little gadget pictured has recognised the would-be driver's fingerprint. Whilst such progress is to be lauded, it is to be hoped that the owner never injures the finger in such a way that a plaster masks the print: computers can in such circumstances be infuriatingly unsympathetic.

BOBBY FINDERS

It may be of some comfort to a 21st-century motorist, contemplating his or her lot as a persecuted breed, to know that it was ever thus. Indeed, the Automobile Association was set up in 1905 specifically to defeat over-zealous policing of motorists breaking the 20mph speed limit.

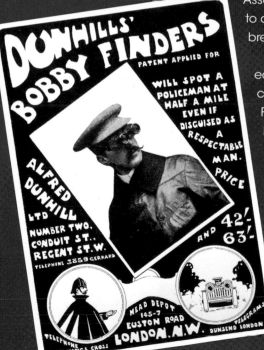

For motorists out of reach of those early AA patrols, Alfred Dunhill's Motorities catalogue for that year offered the Bobby Finders at 42 shillings, which appear to be a pair of modified opera glasses designed to enable the motorist to see further ahead. Of particular interest is the advertising strap-line, which claimed that by wearing them the driver would be able to 'spot a policeman at half a mile, even if disguised as a respectable man.'

Unfortunately, there are no known examples of the Bobby Finders surviving today.

BOLT-ON FINS

Car ownership in 1950s Britain was still a distant dream for millions. For many of those lucky enough to own a car, it represented a huge investment, and was much more highly prized than today's cars are by their owners who regularly change them.

LOTT (Regd. Designs)

INDICATOR REAR FINS & HEADLAMP HOODS WILL COMPLETELY MODERNISE YOUR Mk. I CONSUL, ZEPHYR or ZODIAC

★ PROVIDE SEPARATE AMBER FLASHING INDICATORS IN THE BEST POSITIONS
★ STAINLESS STEEL EMBELLISHMENTS
★ KITS ARE SUPPLIED WITH EVERYTHING FOR EASY FITTING IN A FEW HOURS

Leaflet on request to :

Retail prices from
£8.18.0 PAIR FINS
£8.4.0 PAIR HOODS
INCLUDING LAMPS

D. F. LOTT & Cº LᵀᴰD 161-163 GLOBE ROAD, LONDON, E.2
PHONE : ADVANCE 5422.

For those who could not afford the newest style in late-1950s cars, and were stuck with models from earlier in the decade, a few pounds spent could, if the adverts were to be believed, wreak a transformation. Companies such as Lotts offered bolt-on fins for cars such as the Mk1 (very rounded) Ford Zephyr, which would, they claimed, greatly modernise the old girl.

As an inexpensive way of tarting up old bangers, it is amusing to modern eyes, but surviving examples must be extremely rare.

BOOT
LUGGAGE RACK

It's amazing what a difference to the appearance of a car a boot luggage rack can make. On cars such as the MGB roadster, it transforms the sportscar into a tourer, immediately conjuring up visions of motoring holidays, with a wicker picnic basket strapped to the rack, as you head off towards the horizon.

This simple accessory has been available for decades, and the particular irony is that rather than drawing attention to the car's lack of luggage-carrying capabilities, in most cases it improves its image. Exceptions, however, do exist: cars such as Volvos, Daimlers and the Ford Cortina generally do not benefit from the addition of such an accessory.

BREITLING FOR BENTLEY

It is entirely fitting that one of the greatest marques in motoring should ally itself with a watch manufacturer with a similar heritage of excellence. Both Bentley Motors and Breitling share a winged B signature, and the range of watches offered under the Breitling for Bentley name is every bit as desirable as the cars with which they are linked.

The Bentley Motors T pictured here is equipped with a world-exclusive variable tachometer, enabling measurement of average speed, whatever the time elapsed, the distance covered or the speed reached. Made to the same exacting standards as the Bentley, this self-winding, 38-jewel timepiece is not only a chronometer of unrivalled quality and accuracy, but its elegance displays perfectly the levels of craftsmanship that have gone into making this one of the most desirable motoring watches.

BREXTON 'EVERSAFE' BABY-CHAIR

As modern motorists, we are very aware of the need for safety features in our cars, and protecting particularly vulnerable young children is a major concern. Modern child seats offer high levels of protection in the event of a collision, but this was not always so.

With the benefit of hindsight and superior understanding of safety issues, we can today look with horror at the Brexton 'Eversafe' Baby-Chair of 1968, and wonder if perhaps there is a letter N missing from the beginning of its name. It should, however, be borne in mind that the alternative at that time was simply to allow youngsters to roam freely around the interior of the car, and in this context, it may possibly have offered a limited amount of protection in a very minor accident. Fortunately, we can all say with a huge sigh of relief 'They don't make 'em like that any more.'

BUDDY ON DEMAND

Driving alone at night can be a frightening experience. What a lone girl needs is a male companion, or if not a real one, something that might look like one, sitting in the passenger seat. An Australian insurance company targeting their services at women drivers offer just such a person, albeit an inflatable, rough approximation of one, known and marketed as 'Buddy on Demand'. In the cold light of day 'he' obviously offers the prospect of little back-up support against would-be evil doers and their schemes, but at night, the presence of a body that bears some resemblance to a human male (through squinted glances) might offer the feeling of increased security to the more timid of female drivers.

BULLDOG MASCOT

Over the span of motoring history, there have been countless mascots produced, and singling out examples for inclusion is almost impossible. The bulldog mascot sold by Dunhills in the 1920s, however, is worthy of note not only for its ugliness, but because behind the dark blue glass in the goggles on its face was a little electric light. This must have given it a most bizarre appearance and, interestingly, was a forerunner of the blue-light windscreen washer jets currently adopted by certain hot-hatch owners.

Behind this bulldog mascot's blue glass goggles is mounted an electric light, which produces a weird and rather fascinating effect when current from the batteries is allowed to pass. The bull-dog is excellently modelled, and is designed for attachment to the radiator cap. (Dunhills, Ltd., 359-361, Euston Road, London, N.W.1.)

BULLET HOLES

Among the more perplexing of accessories available to the modern consumer keen to personalise his or her vehicle must surely be stick-on bullet holes. Looking convincingly realistic, the obvious conclusion one might arrive at is that the owner of the vehicle to which they are attached is either particularly unpopular (and is happy for people to know it) or lives in a most undesirable neighbourhood.

   Neither scenario is normally one about which one might feel inclined to boast, and yet the fact that these decals sell must surely suggest that for certain people such claims are indeed badges of honour.

BUMPER DUMPER

Mother Nature can be truly awe-inspiring. The Great Outdoors beckons, and many heed the call to go exploring. She can, however, make other demands of a rather more personal nature at the most inopportune of moments when you are miles from anywhere and such occasions can be deeply distressing.

That is, unless you've thought ahead, and come with the self-explanatory Bumper Dumper, a gadget that quickly attaches to your pick-up truck's tow-hitch for instant relief. Not only can one's comfort be restored in the most picturesque scenery, but without the four walls that normally surround such facilities, one's breath can be taken away by the landscape rather than the quickly dispersed less pleasant odours. Some versions even come with an attached loo-roll holder.

CALL-SAFE CAR PHONE

Before the mid-1980s, car-phones were the stuff of dreams. As mobile telephony became a possibility, luxury car manufacturers rushed to add built-in car phones to their list of expensive options.

This created two things: an aspiration to have a car phone fitted, thus being seen to be among the winners (this was the 1980s, after all), and a desire amongst those who could not justify or afford a car phone to be able to make calls in the case of emergency. For just such people, the good guys at the AA came up with the Call-Safe phone: a car phone with just one option, which connected the anxious caller to the AA in case of a breakdown. For several years, this was available to members of the AA, until mobile phones proliferated and became cheap (and efficient) enough for everyone to afford, at which point, the Call-Safe became obsolete and was withdrawn.

CANINE COVERS PET DOOR SHIELDS

Dogs in cars can be excitable things. The view from a side window, open or shut can be fascinating, demanding the full attention of the beloved pooch. Beloved, that is, until the claws used to gain purchase on the door trim start to damage the car's finish.

A startlingly simple remedy to this problem, and that of accompanying dog hair and general grime is the Canine Covers Pet Door Shield. Sold in pairs, these durable coated polyester fabric covers not only protect the vulnerable car trim, but can be removed and machine washed. Often, the simple solution is just the most brilliant.

CARPORT

The carport offers limited shelter to the cars it protects, but in contrast offers considerably more ventilation than a garage. Its origins can be traced back to the well-known American architect, Frank Lloyd Wright, who coined the phrase when designing a house in 1936. He famously noted that 'A car is not a horse, and it does not need a barn. Cars are well-built enough now that they do not need an elaborate shelter.' Whilst many carports are very simple structures added on to the side of a house, the design of them has varied enormously since their creator's minimalist first offering.

CHROMA FLAIR PAINT

Nissan are no strangers to offering their vehicles in bold colour schemes: they even offered a Cabstar Pickup that one might normally expect builders to buy, in bright pink. The use of Chroma Flair paint on the 1998 Micra, however, was more unusual than most.

Chroma Flair Paint changes colour depending on the levels of light falling on it, using ultra-thin layers of colourless materials to create the different colours through the physics of light interference. This option made the humble little car into something quite spectacular, although owners must surely have worried should the paint ever need repair.

CITIZEN BAND RADIO

Citizen Band (or as it's more popularly known, CB) radio had been going for many years in the US before the 1978 film *Convoy*, a story of renegade truckers and others led by Kris Kristofferson, hit the screens. Invented to combat tedium and loneliness among American truckers on the long journeys, CBs crossed the Atlantic following the famed road-movie.

What added further to the excitement amongst UK users was its illegality, where licences were required, but seldom bought, before the sets could be operated. For a while, no self-respecting Cortina-driving rebel would be without his 'rig', and great excitement would arise if one user 'eyeballed' (saw) another with whom he/she had been communicating. As memories of *Convoy* faded, the CB fad dwindled, although it still has a small contingent of devotees who prefer talking to their 'good buddies' via CB. Most people now, however, prefer the much further-reaching mobile phone as a means of communication.

CITROËN 2CV BOOT EXTENSION

The Citroën 2CV is just about the purest example of motoring simplicity. Whilst it is possible to fit accessories to this unique machine, very few of them ever blend convincingly with the essence of the car, and always appear incongruous, much like adding a conservatory to an office block.

A rare exception is the boot extender, which a variety of manufacturers have offered over the years. What is of particular interest, although to date has not been scientifically verified, is the rumour that the addition of this strange structure to the rear of the car actually increases its top speed by endowing it with slightly improved aerodynamic efficiency. With just 602cc and a maximum of 29bhp available, however, the filling of this increased luggage area with anything weighing much more than a postage stamp is likely to offset any increased ability to cut a path through the air.

COLLAPSIBLE LEATHER BUCKET

Everyone knows that water is essential for life: cars are also pretty dependent on the stuff. With the exception of air-cooled engines, its role in preventing the motive unit from self-destruction through heat build-up is crucial, whilst its cleaning properties for windscreens, headlights etc are self-evident.

In Edwardian days, the chauffeur might well be expected to clean the car whilst awaiting his employer's return from whatever function he or she was attending, and for just such moments, the collapsible leather bucket must have been a godsend. Easy to store when flat, its presence could ensure the car was always spotless, the owner happy and the chauffeur gainfully employed.

DUNHILL'S MOTORITIES

COLLAPSIBLE BUCKETS AND CANS

MOST useful accessories to every car; can be used for petrol, water, or any liquid, avoid all rattle and noise, and can be closed up to carry under the seat. Made from the best double boiled sailcloth canvas.

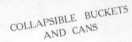

890. Can, handsewn with stout waxed thread 4 6

891. Ditto, second quality 3 0

892. Bucket, first quality 4 6

893. Ditto, second quality 3 0

991. Can, with hose attachment fitted in such a manner that water can be emptied into the tank without being spilled. The nozzle of the hose contains a filter, so that the can may be filled with water from a pond without fear of dirt entering the tank. When not in use the hose is hooked to the handle 8 6

275

COMPETITION SEAT

Fitting sports seats must be one of the easiest, and psychologically most rewarding 'improvements' you can make to a car, endowing it with a greater feeling of sportiness without actually improving its performance at all.

Installing rally or competition seats is no new phenomenon, as this photo from 1969 shows. This purchaser of the fantastically named Karobes Recorde Competition Seat is about to transform, in her own mind, the stature of her humble Mini into something approaching that of a Paddy Hopkirk Monte-winning champion. Other additions might include a smaller steering wheel and a set of 'Carlos Fandango' go-faster super-wide wheels, with fluffy dice dangling from the rear-view mirror to provide that finishing touch.

DIRECTA-SCOPE MIRROR

SEE AT A GLANCE WHETHER YOUR INDICATOR IS UP

Whilst some gadgets are as useful today as when they were first launched, there are many that are time sensitive, and no longer have any use on a modern car. One such accessory is the Directascope Mirror, whose use was to allow the forgetful driver to see whether or not he had cancelled the trafficator arm that all cars were fitted with prior to the introduction of flashing indicators.

DOGGLES

It's a problem that dog-owning motorists, especially those with sportscars or dogs who crave to stick their heads out of the window, have faced since the beginning of motorised transport. Caring for your pooch's eyes in such draughty conditions is not something to be ignored, and from the outset, goggles have been available to alleviate the problem.

Doggles are a modern brand of goggles aimed at man's best friend, and come in a bewildering array of shapes, sizes, and lens options, including clear, smoked and even mirrored for the particularly cool canine.

DRINKS CABINET – IN A SPORTS CAR

While many people will be familiar with the idea of drinks cabinets being fitted to cars - in certain of the larger Rolls-Royce models they were all but compulsory - the fitting of such an accessory to a sports car shows both desperation and almost criminal stupidity in equal measure.

Admittedly it was fitted to the passenger door, but the fitting of a drinks cabinet to the interior of the prototype Alvis TB14, first shown in 1948, illustrates that the manufacturers must have been expecting adverse comments about the car's styling, and decided to install the booze to give the journalists something else to write about. It didn't work, however, as only 100 TB14s were ever built, and none of the customer cars, thankfully, had this particular accessory included in their specification sheets.

DRI-SLEEVE

Whilst the number of clothing manufacturers who have offered motoring coats must be well into the hundreds, only once has a waterproof sleeve on its own been included in the list of equipment for a car.

The year was 1971, and the car, named after its clothing accessory (a unique occurrence in itself) was the Dri-Sleeve Moonraker, built well away from the normal sphere of UK car manufacture, in Warminster, Wiltshire. Styled to imilate the iconic Type 35 Bugatti, the famed single sleeve's purpose was to allow the driver to change gear with the externally placed lever in any weather.

Although the car was extremely well built, sales success completely eluded the company, which folded the same year the car was launched. It is not known whether any cars (or sleeves) survive.

DRIVEMOCION ILLUMINATING SIGN

Modern roads are congested places, where drivers often become frustrated and tempers flare perhaps more easily than they otherwise might. Aggression is a commonplace occurrence, and incidents of road rage are all too commonplace.

What is required is something which would allow drivers to display messages other than those most easily passed on using a couple of fingers. Enter the Drivemocion, a battery-powered rear window display unit which can display any one of a series of pre-programmed messages to drivers behind. Simple designs such as smiling faces, or, as pictured, a word of thanks may help defuse a situation, and it is not programmable to communicate messages other than those installed by the manufacturers.

DRIVER ALERT MASTER

In today's high-pressure world, most of us work harder and longer than we would choose, and often this involves spending long periods at the wheel of a car.

The problem with this is that once the driver is sitting in a warm environment, he or she can often be overwhelmed by drowsiness without being aware of its onset. Each year, many serious accidents happen that are directly attributable to driver fatigue. The Driver Alert Master is a little gadget that sits behind the driver's ear, and should his or her head suddenly nod forward, it will beep loudly to return them to full consciousness. Costing roughly the same price as a gallon of petrol, it is an inexpensive potential lifesaver, but should not be looked on as a licence to press on when too tired to concentrate.

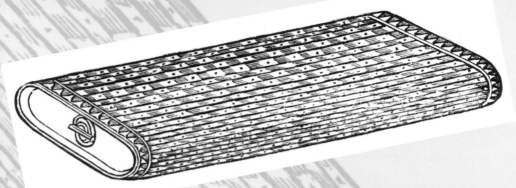

DUCO
OVAL CARPET
WARMER

In the days before global warming, winters could be really quite cold. Cold enough to be seriously uncomfortable, and so it wasn't long before people started to think about remedying the situation for those who needed to venture out in a motor car.

An early device for transferring the heat generated from the engine to a more appreciated zone of the car was the Duco Oval Carpet Warmer from Edwardian days. In common with many devices, its beauty lay in its simplicity. Taking hot water from the cooling system on a slight detour, it sent it via a pipe through the tastefully carpet-wrapped body of the warmer before returning to the engine, warming the feet of the needy passenger en route.

DUST GOGGLES

One of the great problems endured by early motorists, at least in the summer months, was the clouds of dust kicked up by their cars as they made their way along the predominantly gravel roads. So thick and troublesome were the clouds caused that elaborate costumes were sold by all the major fashion houses for anyone considering taking up the new hobby.

Protecting one's eyes from the dust was imperative, and a number of inventive solutions were tried, some with more success than others. One was the goggles featured here, with only the narrowest slits through which the wearer (and bear in mind, that could actually be the driver) was supposed to peer. Eyestrain would doubtless rapidly present itself as a problem for the wearer, if hitting some obstacle on the road had not already removed the need to continue wearing them.

EASYFIT FENDERS

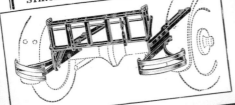

Clumsy and incompetent drivers, it would appear, have been a problem on the roads since the very earliest days, and car parking has always presented such drivers with real problems. Modern cars deal with this by having bumpers that can take low impacts without danger, and increasingly radar is fitted to give more warning of impending contact.

Back in the 1920s, however, Easyfit Fenders offered the best solution to driver ineptitude. Made from either light or heavyweight sprung steel and costing from 30 shillings, they mounted easily to the front or rear of the chassis, allowing you to bounce off walls, trees or other cars, not unlike dodgem cars, without damaging your own car.

ELTRON ELECTRIC CAR KETTLE

The Brits are well known throughout the world as tea-drinkers, and indeed if tea drinking were ever launched as an Olympic sport, there is little doubt that the gold medal would never leave the island's shores.

It should come as no surprise, therefore, to find that for many decades numerous companies have offered electric kettles running from the car's 12-volt system. This Eltron from 1957 is a good example of just such a device, there to ensure that at a moment's notice, a nice steaming hot cuppa can be produced to soothe away the pressures of a long journey, or to savour whilst taking in the beauties of the English countryside.

ELTRON CAR KETTLE
12 VOLT.
Boils while you drive. Takes practically nothing from the battery.

IDEAL FOR A PICNIC CUP OF TEA

1½ PINT POLISHED ALUMINIUM TEAPOT, HEATER, FLEX, PLUG AND SOCKET

ALL COMPLETE including purchase tax **37/3**

Obtainable from your garage or direct from :

ELTRON (LONDON) LTD., STRATHMORE ROAD, CROYDON

Telephone : Thornton Heath 1861

EVERFLEX ROOF

During the 1970s and early 1980s, when vinyl roofs were fashionable, and were a feeble pretence supposed to give the look of a convertible with its hood up, almost every manufacturer sold the more luxurious of their offerings thus bedecked.

   Rolls-Royce Motor Cars, ever keen to present their customers with the best that money could buy, offered their cars similarly adorned, although naturally they opted for the best material for the job. Everflex was a British-made vinyl fabric of superior quality that was considerably more expensive than what was generally used, but it was also more durable. It was fitted to the cars on top of a layer of fabric that padded it slightly and added weight and body, giving the impression of a hood.

EXHAUST FLAME THROWER

Without doubt, one of the world's more unusual car accessories has to be the FlameKitz Exhaust Flame-Thrower kit. Once installed, this handy and relatively inexpensive gadget can turn your passion wagon into a James Bond-esque super chariot.

Installation is apparently none too difficult (its makers spell out, however, the dangers associated with mixing naked flames, electrical circuitry and the many flammable components in a modern car), although its legality is debatable, and ultimately, opportunities to use it cannot be that frequent. As the photo shows, it can nevertheless look highly impressive in the dark.

Undeniably, fixing flamethrowers to a car is all about making a statement: understanding that statement, however, can be a deeply perplexing issue.

EXHAUST PIPE MASCOT

For much of the car's life, the exhaust pipe has been a component largely ignored by stylists and owners alike, treated almost like a car's private parts. Many designs have sought to hide it completely, but in the mid-1930s, those not ashamed of the pipe could elect to decorate it with one of several mascots.

Made from highly polished cast aluminium, several designs were available, including a crocodile, a tiger and even an eagle, as well as this greyhound's head that let the fumes exit through its mouth.

EXHAUST PIPE MASCOTS.

EXHAUST
WHISTLE

One of the most interesting characteristics of veteran and Edwardian cars is the sheer levels of ingenuity employed in their design. Modern cars by and large are the sum of a wealth of accumulated knowledge earned from over a century of experience learning what works well and what doesn't. Early car designers had none of this experience, and it was their trials and errors that ultimately built this bank of knowledge.

One such gem of ingenuity was the exhaust whistle. It was operated by pulling a lever that, by means of a cable running to the rear of the car, shut a sluice, redirecting the flow of exhaust gases through a whistle, and thereby alerting the unaware to the hazards the driver posed.

In theory a great idea, the engine on this car, however, ran slowly (around 1000 rpm) and so the pressure of exhaust gases fluctuated, producing more of a warble than a piercing whistle. On a modern car, however...

2075

2649

2247

2648

FISHING ACCESSORIES

In the West, fishing is predominantly a leisure activity, undertaken by men who have no shed to retreat to. In other parts of the world, however, the fish caught form an integral part of the family diet, and it is viewed with much greater seriousness.

In Russia, for instance, the ZAZ 966, launched in 1967, had such family dietary considerations at heart: not only did the floor have a fishing hole in it, through which the car's occupant could drop a line down and through the frozen lake on which it was parked to attract that evening's supper, but a paraffin heater was also offered as an option to keep the fisherman warm until supper arrived.

FLICKIN' THE BIRD PUMP-UP FINGER

Not everyone on the roads today is a model of good manners and patience. Driving can be a stressful affair, and smiling politely, as the Drivemocion offers, is not for everyone.

For such people, especially those not afraid of the possibility of escalating road-rage, the Flickin' The Bird Pump-Up Finger offers a crude way of expressing displeasure to other drivers. At the moment of highest tension, a quick squeeze of the pump raises the middle finger of the hand held in the car's rear window, and the world is instantly apprised of your feelings. How those offended by such directness are likely to respond, however, is something that should perhaps be addressed before reaching for that pump.

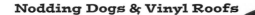

FLUFFY DICE

Surely fluffy dice must rate highly on anyone's list of naff ways of personalising a car, and yet their popularity has remained largely undiminished over several decades, having originally found favour in the 1950s. Not only are they deeply unoriginal, but fitting them must also rate as one of the laziest and least imaginative ways of decorating a car's interior, along with tiger-skin seat covers and steering-wheel covers.

Modern examples can, however, fulfil a useful function in that they may be bought with an air freshener inside. As one major internet retailer of car accessories says of their (de rigueur) pink fluffy dice, 'What more can we say – still one of our best sellers!!!!' How depressing.

FOLD-BACK FABRIC SUNROOF

Many owners of saloon cars wish they had a convertible, something a little racy and yet as practical as the car they ended up choosing. Buying a car so often involves making uncomfortable compromises, and when one has a family, these can be particularly painful.

And yet, they needn't be. For several decades now, it has been possible to own the saloon you know you should have and yet still enjoy most of the pleasures of wind-in-the-hair motoring that can normally be had only by removing the roof. A fold-back fabric sunroof such as those made by Webasto has bridged the gap between sensible and fun for many saloon car owners, turning their compromise car into something much nearer the dream than they may have ever dared to hope.

FUEL ATOMISER

Cars have never been cheap to run, and from the very earliest of days, owners, manufacturers and charlatans alike have sought to reduce the costs of consumables such as fuel.

Obviously, ensuring that the car is in fine tune has to be the first step to ensuring maximum efficiency, but there have always been a variety of gadgets available that claim significantly to boost yet further the car's efficiency. Such promises were made of this fuel atomiser from 1955, descendants of which can still be bought today. The idea behind this little gadget is simple; its effectiveness is highly questionable.

The question any would-be purchaser might well ask themselves before introducing such a gadget to the car is, "If it works that well, why didn't the car's manufacturer specify it as standard fit from new?"

Chatwin Rotary Atomiser

WORLD PATENTS APPLIED FOR

= { Better performance
Saving in petrol
Reduced engine wear

The initial cost of this amazing Atomiser can be saved in petrol in the first 2,000 miles after fitting. Ask your local garage for more detailed information.

Retail Price 57/6
Dual Type £5.10.0

Motor Cycle type for all models of 350 c.c. and over, 43/6.

Easily fitted with all standard carburettors.

Sole distributors :

J. HOLLIS & SON
51/53 PARK STREET, BIRMINGHAM, 5
TELEPHONE : MIDLAND 4965

GAS BAG

With the outbreak of war in 1939, motorists across Europe rapidly found that their normal freedom to drive wherever they pleased was dramatically curtailed, and for many, car ownership meant nothing more meaningful than looking in the lock-up garage at the slowly rusting machine that had been laid up 'for the duration'.

Car ownership, however, is a deeply addictive condition for many people, and the inventive few who could not bear to be parted from their cars started to look at making alternative fuels to keep them going. Methane gas, refined from, among other things, chicken droppings, was tried, with the gas being stored in a huge sack fixed to the roof, but success can, at best, be viewed as moderate.

GRADIENT METER

For several generations, motorists have looked at the hill on the road ahead without much real concern. Such could not be said for the early drivers, whose vehicles often struggled to climb the steeper gradients, especially if 'the old girl' was not in an excellent state of tune.

Evidence of this can be seen in adverts placed in magazines of the time, such as this, placed in the *Trade Manual* published by Brown Brothers in 1914 for the Gradient Meter. This little gadget allowed the motorist to determine the state of tune of his engine by the length of time taken and amount of effort required to climb a regularly used hill.

In an age of computer-controlled engines, where the state of tune can be altered every 1/100th of a second in the ECU (Electronic Control Unit), such a state of hit-or-miss reliability is hard to imagine.

GUN SAFE

Handgun ownership in the UK is largely limited to enthusiasts and the criminal classes, but in the USA, millions of guns are legitimately privately owned. For many Americans, carrying a handgun gives them both a sense of identity and security, but obviously while you're driving, it's best to put it down somewhere safe.

To solve just such conundrums you can buy a console vault that fits concealed in the centre console between the two front seats. Made from 12-gauge cold-rolled plate steel, and featuring welded tab and notch seams, bank-vault style hinge latch pins, and a three-point locking system, with the console closed this must be just about the safest place to keep a gun...

...which is a bit like saying that driving with bald tyres is perfectly OK if you brake carefully on dry roads only.

HAND LAMP

The night poses many dangers, the biggest surely being the inability to see much without illumination. Whilst in modern times we are able to buy torches with the power to light seemingly half of London, the early motorist was not so lucky, not least because battery technology was still in its infancy.

As if to show that there is very little that is truly new, clockwork-powered torches were being sold by companies such as Alfred Dunhill, Gamages and others after the First World War. The amount of light given off from them as illustrated was probably somewhat exaggerated, however, and cramp would set in quite quickly when operating such devices.

HEADLAMP BLACKOUT VISORS

The Blackout Visor, as specified at the outbreak of the Second World War, may have been necessary as part of the blackout, but it must surely have been the single most dangerous accessory ever sold.

Official statistics back this claim, as it is a known fact that more people were killed on the roads of Britain in 1939 as a result of the blackout regulations than died that year in active combat. And that was with the numbers of vehicles using the roads reduced to essential users only, because of petrol rationing.

STARLIGHT HEADLINER

Designing a new car can be a tricky enough job for any manufacturer, but when your name is Rolls-Royce, the expectations upon you to raise the bar to new levels of luxury and excellence are extraordinarily high.

So when the company unveiled its experimental car, the 101EX in February 2006, the world waited eagerly to see what new wonders would greet future owners of any car that might follow this experimental model. Among a wealth of dazzling equipment and luxurious fittings was the Starlight Headliner, made up of hundreds of fibre-optic cables embedded in the leather headlining to give the impression of a star-filled night sky. Whilst no-one can claim this greatly advances the design of cars, its beauty and contribution to an atmosphere of unrivalled opulence mark it out as something of a milestone in car-interior desirability.

HORSTMANN KICK-STARTER

There have doubtless been times in the lives of most motorists when they have been sorely tempted to kick the car they are driving, or perhaps trying to drive. In the case of early Horstmann cars, built by a German clockmaker who set up business in Bath before the First World War, kicking the car was the means of starting it.

The kick-start mechanism operated on an Archimedes screw on the prop-shaft, as can be seen in the photograph, and must make it one of the most unusual ways of coaxing a car into life.

HUNTING SEAT

Thankfully, the number of individuals likely to look for an electro-hydraulic-powered hunting seat that will lift its occupant through the folded back sunroof to take a pot-shot at some passing wildlife is remarkably few.

There will always be a market for such irrelevant extravagances, however, and for people who required this in the 1970s, companies such as Rapport International existed, converting stretched Range Rovers into gin palaces, mainly for Arab clients. Whilst the self-elevating seats were perhaps the most obvious symbols of pretentious opulence, faux pram irons fixed to the C-Pillars ensured that everyone realised that this was most definitely not done 'in the best possible taste.'

The 'COLLITE' MAGNIFIER
for MAP READING

It Magnifies
& Illuminates

The unbreakable white Polythene housing holds 2½in. dia. high quality lens. Height 4½in. Handle takes No. 8 battery and can be used separately as a torch. Red, Blue, Mauve, Green or Gold handles. Torch, lamp and battery. Complete.

20/-
Post Free.

ILLUMINATED MAP FINDER

In the days before sat-navs or Navirobos (Japan only – see page 74), drivers still needed to find their way around unfamiliar areas at night, and a variety of ingenious gadgets was offered to make the task a little easier. One of these was the Collite Illuminated Map Finder, whose simplicity must have won it many friends among those tempted to buy one.

Unlike a sat-nav or Navirobo, using such a gadget offered no promise of getting you to your destination, but did allow you to experience the full frustration of realising how completely lost you had allowed yourself to become.

INSTANT ROOF RACK

Holidays are difficult times, especially for the person charged with cramming unfeasible amounts of luggage into the insufficient boot-space. Roof racks are the traditional solution to this problem, but not only are they unsightly, they also increase drag, which adds to the fuel bill.

Step forward Autolux, whose Autorak instant roof rack, launched in 1980, provided not only the solution to the baggage problem, but was also small enough to be removed and stored in the boot once the car had arrived at the holiday destination. Although good in theory, unless the paintwork was meticulously cleaned before placing the Autorak directly onto it, the en-route vibration could wreak havoc with the paint-surface on which it sat.

KERBFINDERS

Some of the cleverest of gadgets are amongst the simplest in design, and there is perhaps no better example than the K-L Kerbfinder that was popular in the UK towards the end of the 1950s.

In essence, it was little more than a piece of springy steel wire that fitted to the trailing edge of the nearside front wings (although those particularly poor at parking may also have felt tempted to fit them to the rear of the car). Reaching down to kerb level, it would scrape against the kerbstones as the car approached, and its vibrations would be audible inside the car before damage could be done to the tyres by mounting the kerb.

It should be borne in mind that at that time, there was no MOT test, and many cars were driving around on the most fragile and worn-out of tyres. Viewed in such a light, a gadget that preserved the tyres a little longer, and which cost so little to buy was considered a good idea.

PROTECT YOUR TYRES !
K-L KERBFINDERS give warning when kerbs or obstructions are near. No electrical wiring. Price per pair 9/-.

KIDDYPROOF DOOR HANDLES

Possibly because children have never had much of a role in car purchase, they have traditionally rated low in the table of priorities for car designers. Making cars reliable, then comfortable and pleasurable would seem to have been uppermost in the minds of their creators in the battle to win customers.

Children, however, are both mischievous and inquisitive, and when sitting in the back of a car on a long journey, many have been tempted to play with things they should not. Like the door handles, for instance. Whilst modern cars have childproof locks fitted universally as standard, back in 1957 this was not the case. A number of companies therefore offered a variety of gadgets such as these Kiddyproof door handles that the caring parent could fit to make the car slightly safer for the little dears.

LALIQUE MASCOT

Highly sought after by art-lovers and car enthusiasts alike, the glass mascots of René Jules Lalique are among the most beautiful pieces of sculpture ever to grace the radiator grilles of any car.

His first commission came in 1925, from André Citroën for his Cinq Chevaux (5hp) model, and featured five prancing horses in a line. There was a total of 27 different designs, and his inspirations drew on the Art Deco style of the time, alongside other Japanese and far-eastern influences.

LEAPING CAT JAGUAR MASCOT

As many people doubtless know, the proud marque of British sportscars and luxury cars, Jaguar, grew from the small concern, Swallow Sidecars, a company originally set up in Blackpool making stylish sidecars for motorcycles in the years following the First World War. They graduated to making

sportscars, including the iconic SS100, but as the 1930s rolled on, the initials SS took on a less wholesome significance in Europe and, not wishing it to be confused with elements of the growing German military, owner Bill Lyons changed the name to Jaguar.

A mascot depicting the lithe cat was produced, but Lyons rapidly grew tired of its aesthetic impurity, claiming it 'looked like a cat shot off a fence', and the legendary *Autocar* artist, Frederick Gordon Crosby was asked for his version. Although no longer fixed to the bonnets of the Coventry cars on the grounds of safety, this Crosby-styled mascot remains the company's proud mascot to this day, and has become an instantly recognisable trademark.

LEOPARD SKIN RUG

Whilst today, one would automatically assume that anything that looked like leopard skin was faux, in decades gone by, such assumptions were unsafe.

The 'Snuggery' leopard skin rug on sale in the 1920s was made from real ex-leopard. Such rugs may be offensive to 21st-century tastes, largely because leopards and their like are now considerably less common than they once were, and modern imitation furs look every bit as convincing as the real skin.

Fashions (as the leopard will happily note) change, and it is now widely held that by far the best place to see a leopard skin is on the back of a leopard rather than the lap of a wealthy motorist.

DUNHILL'S MOTORITIES

THE "SNUGGERY"

THE luxurious comfort of the "Snuggery"—a form of rug specially contrived for car use—is gratefully appreciated in the piercing wind which searches all nooks and crannies of the car for entrance. It completely envelops the lower portion of the body, terminating in a warm foot-muff, and is so cut as to cosily protect the chest. Warm fur-lined pockets are provided for the hands, and the penetration of wind or cold is absolutely impossible.

229

229A. Handsomely made in leopard skin, lined opossum - 14 Gns.

229. Pony skin, lined black lamb's wool - 9 Gns.

229A

161

LIGHTINSIGHT

The head of the queue at the traffic lights is no bad place to be. With the arrival of the green light, the open road beckons. However, seeing the lights change can be a problem, as the angle of vision can sometimes be too great.

LightInSight is a clear, windscreen-mounted Fresnel lens for assisting drivers in seeing traffic lights not in the driver's normal field of view. Once attached, it brings into view the lights that might otherwise be invisible, and means you don't have to wait for the embarrassing sound of horns from cars behind, alerting you to the fact that your turn has come.

MAGNETIC RIDE DAMPING

The modern car is a fantastically complex machine, with more computing power aboard (allegedly) than was crammed into the first Lunar Module. These computers perform all sorts of unseen tasks, such as those that control the magnetic damping ride option available on cars like the new Audi TT.

This is a feature centred around the dampers (in years gone by they would have been called shock-absorbers) filled with a magnetorheological fluid containing minute magnetic particles that can be influenced by an electromagnetic field. The computer senses the amount of suspension damping required, and by applying electric current to this fluid, the particles instantly alter the viscosity of the fluid, and with it, its damping characteristics.

MASSAGING SEATS

Modern cars are suited to modern life, and often we are faced with travelling long distances to meetings, or even the in-laws. And at the end of a long, often stressful journey, a massage is what's most needed to revive the flagging spirits.

Unless, that is, you've made the journey in the front seats of a Mercedes–Benz S Class. The pampered driver and front passenger of these luxo-barges are lucky enough to ride on seats fitted with separate air chambers in the backrest which are successively inflated and deflated at the touch of a button, massaging the back muscles for the wellbeing of its occupant. The intensity and speed of the massage function can be adjusted in four stages by means of the car's hyper-intelligent COMMAND system.

The perfect car may not yet have arrived, but with such indulgences, it must now surely be close.

MATT BLACK BONNET

Definitely one of the go-faster accessories, which endow the car with the appearance of perhaps greater power than is really present, painting one's bonnet matt black, or in cases such as Ford's Mk1 Capri, specifying it as a factory option, came from motorsport practice.

The end of the 1960s saw a number of truly marathon rallies, including the London–Mexico rally, and even a London–Sydney event. In such feats of endurance, the works teams went to endless efforts to try and preserve their drivers' levels of energy, and reducing glare from the sunlight bouncing off the car's bonnet was seen as a good thing to do.

In no time at all, boy racers and would-be rally drivers up and down the land sprayed their bonnets black, keen to be associated with their heroes and their cars. This must rank as one of the most cost-effective ways of 'improving' the car's appearances, as even those of limited skill could achieve passable results.

MECHANICAL HAND-SIGNALLER

In days gone by, winters were sometimes really, really cold. Coincidentally, these were also the days before cars had conformed to a uniform set of signals to inform drivers behind of your intentions. This meant that if you intended to turn either left or right, or slow down, it was your duty to wind down the window, stick your hand out (with or without gloves), and give the appropriate signal.

In this context, it is perhaps easy to understand why various mechanical signalling devices such as this one illustrated were marketed, although operating them was fiddly and difficult. With the benefits of hindsight, this is another example of why flashing orange lights and bright red brake lights make such good sence.

MUSICAL AIR-HORNS

Devotees of *The Dukes of Hazard* will be familiar with the rebellious fun that can be had from a set of musical air-horns blaring triumphantly as the car screeches away from trouble.

Although illegal on any vehicle made since 1973, they are enjoying something of a comeback with a wide range available at various internet sites, playing the full repertoire of tunes including *Dixie*, *Cavalry Charge*, *Tequila*, *Godfather* et al.

NAVIROBO

Sat-nav systems can be very impersonal, no matter how charming or humorous the voice is. For long journeys, having a car give directions may be helpful, but it could also be lonely.

If you're someone who craves company in such a situation, the Navirobo Teddy Bear (currently only available in Japan) is possibly for you. This cuddly little bear with a slightly disturbing electro-wart on its forehead has a GPS module crammed where other bears have fluff and love. Once placed on the dashboard Navirobo will point you in the correct direction and dance when you arrive at the final destination. Embarrassingly, if you miss a turn he will even laugh at you, which can surely do little for your self-esteem.

THE "NEPTUNE" PORTABLE BATH

A^N ingeniously arranged collapsible bath, of the finest waterproof, constructed to fit into a specially large valise, overlapping the rim, and when filled forms an ideal bath. When folded it occupies only a few inches of space, and the valise will also carry a spare tyre and tubes, etc.

2291. Price of bath only £1 3 0

Price of valises according to size.

NEPTUNE PORTABLE BATH

Early motorists faced a wide variety of trials on every journey they made. Apart from the basic reliability of the car itself (many motorists would think little of regrinding or replacing engine valves mid-journey), a regular trial which faced them was that of punctures. In part the result of poor tyres and in part the fault of bad road surfaces that hid many thousands of horse-hoof nails, a puncture could be expected on most journeys.

A puncture repair kit, including rubber vulcaniser was therefore a part of every motorist's tool kit, and Dunhill's Motorities catalogue added to this the Neptune Portable Bath. Doubling up as a spare wheel cover, it could be removed and filled with water, so that the puncture in the damaged inner tube could be found and repaired more easily than by having to wade in the nearest river, thus allowing the journey to continue with that bit less fuss.

NIGHT VIEW ASSIST

Night-time driving is inherently more dangerous than under daylight conditions, and much time and effort have been invested over the years to try and reduce the dangers. Amongst the newest, high-tech answers is an idea that comes from Mercedes-Benz, inheritors of the title of inventor of the car itself.

Called Night View Assist, the system uses infra red to look ahead, and projects a black & white image onto an 8-inch screen in the centre of the dash. The beauty of using infra red is that the system is not affected by the glare of oncoming headlights, and this must therefore be seen as a great leap forwards. Currently only an option on the most expensive cars in the range, if successful it will doubtless become more widely available in the years to come.

NODDING DOG

The nodding dog is an element of British kitsch every bit as wedded to motoring folklore as roadside cafes, traffic lights and breakdowns. Originally popular in the 1950s, these little fripperies, the motoring equivalent of garden gnomes, sat nodding quietly away on the rear parcel-shelves of cars, animated by the motion of the car. In recent years, the vogue for such canine naffery was revived courtesy of an advertising campaign for an insurance company who have a British Bulldog as their mascot, and who gave away many thousands of them as promotional gifts.

ON-BOARD COMPUTER

Those who believe that computers are a thing of the modern age would be badly mistaken, especially concerning on-board computers fitted to cars. In 1928, the American firm Duesenberg launched their peerless Model J, and this ultimate luxury car came complete with what was known as a timing box. Driven by the fuel-pump shaft, this had warning lights, one of which came on every 700 miles to warn the driver of the need for an oil change, while another came on every 1400 miles to request a battery level check. It also actuated automatically the greasing of all the chassis grease points every 75 miles.

OZONE AIR PURIFIER

As we all know, the interior of a car is not always the most pleasantly scented of places. All sorts of smells, from the plastics in the cabin to the fish and chips wrapper conspire to make some car interiors a full-on nasal assault zone.

Traditionally, owners have resorted to air fresheners that come in a bewildering array of designs from the functional to the humorous, but now there is a scientific alternative: the ozone purifier. Ozone works chemically to reduce at molecular levels the odours that trouble us, turning them into carbon dioxide, water and oxygen. Depending on which research you choose to believe, ozone can be either beneficial or detrimental to health if used in large amounts.

PARKING GODDESS

Definitely one for the gullible, this 2½-inch-high figure is supposed to guide its owner magically to the nirvana of all urban drivers: the perfect parking space. Once fixed by the accompanying adhesive to the car's dash, she just needs to be wound up to set her on her quest. She will then flap her wings as she performs her divine trick. Made of shiny silver plastic, it would surely be most depressing if anyone bought her earnestly believing in her 'powers', although the fact that the back of the card features a prayer to offer to the goddess for best results suggests that for some, purchasing her is indeed an act of faith – or perhaps desperation.

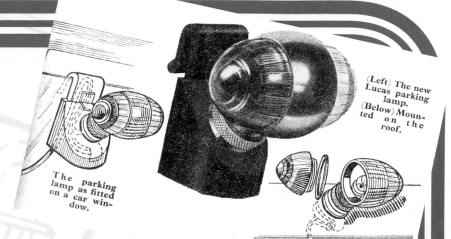

The parking lamp as fitted on a car window.

(Left) The new Lucas parking lamp.
(Below) Mounted on the roof.

PARKING LAMP

Modern cars come equipped with heavy-duty batteries well up to the task of powering the car's sidelights for several hours without detriment, but this was not always the case. Battery technology has come a long way.

Previous generations used to worry about leaving the old girl parked on blind bends or in shaded areas, unlit and a real danger, until companies such as Joseph Lucas came up with the Parking Lamp, as illustrated. Having just one low-wattage lamp, its demands on the car's battery were meagre, and this little device played a worthwhile role in increasing road safety. Nowadays, we simply leave the sidelights on.

PHOTO-BLOCKER SPRAY

One of the hazards facing the modern driver is the ever-growing number of automated tax collectors, known more widely as Gatsos, or speed cameras. The huge number of drivers who suffer sullied licences and lightened wallets courtesy of these devices grows each year, which logically must mean not only that they are failing spectacularly to encourage drivers to slow down, but are also succeeding beyond the wildest dreams of avarice in cash generation.

It is not surprising, therefore, that drivers look to anything that might reduce their chances of joining the vast photographic library that is the rogues' gallery, and one such simple solution is the PhotoBlocker spray, available on the internet. It claims to provide anti-flash protection by reflecting all of the light from the flash, thus ruining the photo taken by the machine. As with most miracle cures for the evils of life, such claims need to be closely scrutinised, and no guarantees of penalty avoidance are offered by its manufacturers. The best means of avoiding the unwelcome attention of plod paparazzi must always be to travel at speeds unlikely to awaken their automated tyrants.

PICNIC
SET

In the modern world, we are used to eating on the move. Picnics no longer have the sense of occasion they once had, decades ago. Back then, before the Second World War, a trip to the country was something of an adventure, and the idea of taking all the food and necessary equipment for a meal in the glorious countryside had great appeal.

Picnic-sets such as this, offered in the Dunhill's Motorities catalogue from 1926 catered for just such occasions, ensuring that no eventuality one might encounter in trying to take the perfect meal into the Edenesque surroundings would require even the slightest compromise of comfort, or indeed, of etiquette. Such attitudes are unfortunately no longer widespread.

PICNIC TRAY

Car interiors are cosy places, generally. Designed to make the process of travelling as pleasant, comfortable and safe as possible, the seats all face the same way (forwards), and there is usually ample legroom to ensure the journey passes in as much comfort as possible.

They are not always ideal places in which to eat picnics, however. Whilst manufacturers such as Raydot were offering picnic trays that fitted to the inside of the car door as far back as the 1930s, the most stylish solution to the problem was the fitting of beautifully veneered walnut tables that folded away into the rear of the front seats. One car so equipped was none other than the Austin Allegro Van den Plas.

PINK INTERIOR

The Ford Capri Mk1, launched in 1968, was a bold car, built to open an entirely new market sector, which it did very well. It was smart, affordable, easy to drive with hints of its American cousin the Mustang about it, and in certain guises, was tolerably fast.

In short, it had everything it needed to be a sales success; except that someone within the company thought it was missing a trick, and managed to persuade the guys in production to offer it with an interior in pink. It is difficult to imagine what corporate misjudgement allowed this option to go all the way through to production, but very few cars actually left the

PIPE & CIGARETTE SMOKER'S COMPANION SET

In generations gone by, smoking was seen as a sophisticated activity, with huge numbers of people indulging. Cigarettes and pipes were part of many people's lives, and before the health risks were finally widely acknowledged, the need for restraint was not apparent.

This Wilmot Pipe & Smoker's Companion from 1926 reflects the attitudes of the times, making it easy for drivers and passengers in cars to continue merrily smoking their health away. Such accessories were far from uncommon in those days, nor indeed were the tobacconist shops that provided the smoking requisites, and which have now all but completely disappeared.

POCKET ROUTE MAP

In today's world of satellite navigation, where it is supposedly impossible to get lost, it is interesting to note that a full century earlier, similar technology was available. Without the satellites, of course.

Manufactured by Tufnell, the Pocket Route Map was a simple, clockwork device, and was widely advertised within the admittedly still small motoring press. A map on a scroll would slowly wind past the window in the front, revealing the relevant part of the pre-planned journey, and if the motorist should want to stop for any reason, the progress of the scrolling could be similarly arrested. A number of different routes could be purchased on rolls and by inserting them in the mechanism, the intrepid explorer could set off on lengthy journeys, slightly more confident of arrival at the chosen destination.

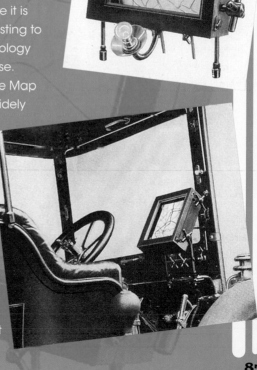

POP-UP SPOILER

The problem with aerodynamics is that at different speeds, different settings are needed for optimum efficiency.

Nowhere is this more obvious than with the rear spoiler, whose principal purpose is to provide extra down-force when the car is travelling at speed. At lower speeds, however, not only is this extra down-force not needed but the spoiler creates drag which reduces fuel efficiency for no real benefit beyond pose. Many manufacturers of performance cars, such as Porsche (pictured) and Bentley are now fitting pop-up devices in an attempt to have the best of both worlds. These lie flat with the bodywork at normal speeds, and pop up only when the car reaches speeds where a spoiler will benefit its stability.

If set correctly, however, its presence in the upright position offers traffic police further visual proof that the car is speeding, as they are normally only efficient above 75mph.

POWERED WINDOWS

Mechanically operated windows were first seen on a Packard in 1919, and it was therefore only going to be a matter of time before someone thought of fitting electric motors to replace the crank-handles that are so tiresome to operate.

Once that had happened, the idea started moving slowly down from the ultra-expensive cars to more mundane machinery, and by 1964, Smiths Industries were offering such technology to most manufacturers, as seen here. Such gadgetry would cost the manufacturers relatively little to install, but allowed for huge profit margins, as the luxury option appeared in sales brochures initially only for the top-of-the-range models.

RAYFLECTA SPOTLIGHT

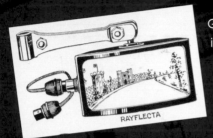

RAYFLECTA

Gadgets have always been cool, especially if they do more than one thing. The Rayflecta Spotlight was available to motorists of the 1920s, who had three separate reasons to like it. Firstly, its convex mirror was a useful size, measuring 6ins x 3ins. Secondly, it had a spotlight built into the front plane: modern cars are now finally taking up this theme and putting indicator repeater lamps in the housings of door mirrors, and thirdly, the space inside housed spare bulbs.

Bearing in mind that spare parts were less readily available and conversely more likely to be required than with modern cars, this last feature was a particularly handy use of the space, and made the Rayflecta a truly useful gadget, although at 57 shillings and sixpence it was by no means cheap.

RAYFLECTA

REAR NUMBER-PLATE CAMERA

The amount of high-tech gadgetry in a modern car is staggering, with computers controlling and monitoring most of the mechanical and electrical functions. And yet, there is still scope for further involvement.

Take for instance, this tiny video camera mounted into the rear number-plate surround, which allows the inept reverser to watch a small screen mounted on the dash and know when to stop rather than wait for the inevitable bump that tells him or her that they can go no further back.

It could be argued that the use of such technology, which allows poorly-trained drivers to continue on their merry way without having to face the consequences of their inadequacy does little to improve the ability of those who most need it, but if it reduces accidents, it can't be all bad.

REAR-VIEW MIRROR

Strange though it may seem, there was a time before cars had rear-view mirrors fitted, and worryingly, as most seasoned drivers will testify, there are some drivers at large today who are still unaware of its presence in the modern car.

Whilst it is impossible to prove beyond all dispute, it is widely believed that veteran motorists were first able to buy an articulated mirror for installation on their cars from the Dunhill's Motorities catalogue in 1902, invented by Dudley Percival and subsequently patented. With so few cars actually on the road in those very early days, however, one would assume that the chance of catching a fellow motorist in one's mirror on the open road must surely have been minimal.

DASHBOARD MIRROR.

With universal joint. Very useful when driving in traffic and turning corners. This mirror, being made with a reducing glass, gives a wide view of the road behind.

1779 ... ... 20/-

RECORD PLAYER

Available for a short while under the attractively snappy name of the Auto-Mignon AG2101 record reproducer, this gadget, on sale for a couple of years at the end of the 1960s, allowed the driver to play 7" single records by simply inserting the disc, in much the same way as most modern CD players work.

Such a gadget, however, was laden with a variety of problems, principal amongst which was that the player's needle had to be heavily weighted to prevent it from bouncing around whilst the car was in motion. This meant that the life of any record played on it was destined to be particularly short, and from the driver's perspective, having to change the record every 3 or 4 minutes must surely have become rapidly tiresome.

Much better, the trendy music-loving type could tune into the newly launched Radio 1, or invest in either an early tape-cassette player or 8-track stereo.

RED FLAG

Without doubt, the accessory least desired was that foisted upon the first UK motorists: the red flag complete with a man walking in front of the car waving it to alert other road users of the impending arrival.

First imposed in 1865 by The Light Locomotives on Highways Act, it was originally intended for steam engines to prevent them from travelling at a speed that would do further damage to Britain's pitifully maintained roads. Early motorists, however, were similarly constrained, a notable example being John Henry Knight, the designer and builder of Britain's first petrol-driven car. On an early journey on his contraption (which happily still exists and is on display at the National Motor Museum, Beaulieu), he was fined five shillings in October 1895 for travelling at the highly irresponsible speed of 8mph, and having neither traction engine licence or flag-waving swaggerer some distance in front.

Happily, this particular accessory became redundant on 14th November 1896, and the annual London–Brighton Run commemorates the first such outing held on that day to celebrate the new speed limit: now a heady 14mph.

RETRACTABLE HARDTOP

Retractable hardtops are now commonplace, but the idea, originally made a reality pre-Second World War by Peugeot for their 601, and recently resurrected, had lain idle for decades since it disappeared at the beginning of the 1960s.

The Ford Motor Co. in the US produced the first mass-produced car fitted with a roof that disappeared, literally at the touch of a button, into its huge trunk (or as it is known in the UK, boot). It was called the Fairlane Skyliner Retractable, and named after Henry Ford's home, Fairlane. While modern systems are the model of reliability (usually!), the Skyliner required the car to be parked on perfectly flat ground if its army of motors, solenoids, micro-switches, and huge lengths of cabling were to perform their impressive disappearing trick on demand and without hitch.

ROCKING DANCER

The principal role of the rear-view mirror (assuming it is properly adjusted) is one of safety, allowing the driver to see the desperate idiot behind swerving and diving, trying to overtake, eager to make his move at the least appropriate moment.

Collectors of kitsch, however, have an altogether more useful purpose for the mirror, as the perfect location from which to suspend trinkets and tat. The truly discerning post-modern humorist will always opt for the bizarre, and this 'Rocking Dancer' complete with gyrating hips (everyone knows it's meant to be Elvis, but the manufacturers daren't call him that for fear of infringing copyright) must surely rate amongst the cheesiest of in-car ornaments. Those with an advanced sense of irony or little self-esteem can still purchase them today.

SAABO CARAVAN

Among the myriad of options and accessories offered by mainstream manufacturers, a caravan to go with the car is probably unique to Saab. Called the Saabo, it was on sale for just four years from 1964 onwards, during which time fewer than 500 examples sold.

Prettiness was not one of its attributes: it had large, low-set windows at the front and rear to allow the driver of the towing vehicle (a Saab, perchance?) to see right through it in the rear view mirror, and was made from two half shells of glassfibre. It was insulated from the Swedish cold with folded cardboard, and LPG was used for the cooking, heating and even lighting. In spite of its diminutive size, it was designed to sleep four people, and clever packaging allowed for two sofas, two wardrobes, a galley sink and even a dining table to be squeezed inside. Happily there are surviving examples.

SEAT COVERS

Once cars started to become reliable enough that their lifespan extended beyond their first or second owners, a number of components started wearing out and needing repair or replacement.

Amongst the most visible of such items must surely have been the seats, which from new would have been clothed in leather, leatherette or cloth. With constant use, these coverings would naturally deteriorate, and so from an early date, the market for made-to-measure seat covers enjoyed a steady stream of custom from impecunious owners of older cars unwilling to recover the seats properly.

The range of materials and patterns offered over the years has been truly bewildering, from imitation leopard skin to shocking pink fur, all boasting a supposed increase in luxury and ambience within the car. This market is as alive today as it has ever been.

THE **First** NAME IN CAR SEAT COVERS!

Regency

'**My! how smart we are!**'

We couldn't be smarter—
now we have Regency Covers

SHOPPING TROLLEY

With constant competition from rivals, vehicle manufactures have to aim not only to offer the best in class, but also often rely on what might appear as gimmicks to steal a march over the competition.

When Citroën launched the Xsara Picasso in 2001, competition in the mini MPV sector was already stiff. Apart from producing a great lifestyle vehicle, they added a little bonus in the boot – a foldaway shopping trolley. It may seem a trivial accessory, but it demonstrates admirably how when the going gets tough, the tough have to get resourceful. The shopping malls may not be full of proud Picasso owners charging round with their branded trolleys, but Citroën had a little extra with which to attract customers.

SNAKE HORN

The Edwardian era was an age of glamour, and in motoring design, it produced some outstanding and startling pieces of folly which have never since been repeated.

For some of the grander vehicles, one adornment which could add the finishing touch was a large bulb-horn which transmitted its bellow down a long and flexible tube to a menacing head that looked like a cross between a snake's and an anaconda's head.

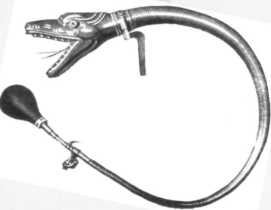

Available through, among others, the Dunhill's Motorities catalogue, it might not have been the noisiest device on sale, but it gave the car onto which it was fixed an added air of menace. Cars of this period were unbelievably expensive, and such a device would add further to its mystique.

SNOW PLOW

Enemies of 4x4s wrongly blame these capable go-anywhere vehicles for many of the world's climate irregularities, when if they looked a little further, they would see just how useful a car that needs no road can be.

Far away from any evidence of global warming, when the snow is thick and the roads are all blocked, a 4x4 fitted with the SnowSport Snow Plow – a feat that takes very little time – could quite literally save the day. Then mummy can once again use the 4x4 to deliver junior to school.

SPEED INDICATOR

Knowing reliably what speed you are travelling at was every bit as important at the dawn of motoring as it is today, and for the same reason: speed traps. Having a gauge for indicating speed was not a legal requirement before the First World War, however, and a range of after-market gadgets was offered to meet this need.

One such was The Warner Patent Magnetic Speed Indicator, about which its makers made some pretty bold claims. It would, for instance, register up to 60mph, was made like a watch, was completely dustproof (very important at a time when dusty roads were the norm), and was 'completely infallible' below 10mph. What part the magnets played remains unexplained.

SPEED NYMPH

Often mistakenly thought of as being in some way related to Rolls-Royce's peerless Spirit of Ecstasy mascot that was modelled in 1910 by Eleanor Thornton and sculpted by the renowned Edwardian artist, Charles Sykes, the Speed Nymph mascot was widely available, and was not marque specific.

Sold as an accessory by a number of manufacturers throughout the 1920s, the addition of such a figure to a relatively humble car (of which there were a great many different marques producing relatively small numbers before the Stock Market crash of 1929) would give it an air of greater sophistication and desirability than might otherwise have been easily obtained. Furthermore, when the car was sold, often the mascot would be held on to, and passed down through subsequent generations of the family, invariably gaining perceived significance with each change of ownership. It is thus easy to see why they turn up in the hands of hopefuls on TV antiques shows, with current owners keen to boast of their family heirloom status, with grand stories attached to them.

SPOILER

It is ironic that the name spoiler, whilst meant to refer to the effect they have on undesirable air-paths over the car, so often aptly describes the aesthetic effect such devices have on the appearance of the car to which they have been fitted.

Perhaps no better example can be seen than in this 'Speed Spoiler' the witless Ford Capri owner desperate to impress could purchase back in 1970. It was presumably meant to redirect airflow over the windscreen, although a modern aerodynamicist would most likely prove it to be inefficient in that task. It also failed in endowing the Capri with more aggressive looks, and very few were sold.

ST CHRISTOPHER MASCOT

Among his portfolio of patronage, St Christopher is responsible for transport, storms, epilepsy, bookbinders, archers, fruit-dealers and toothache. Little is known about the man, as stories concerning his life differ greatly and much of his life is based in legend, but it is believed he was martyred in AD 251.

Long before the invention of the car, St Christopher was revered as the patron saint for long journeys, and so his appearance on mascots and medals hanging from the rear-view mirror to invoke protection for journeys is of little surprise. Pictured is a particularly fine radiator mascot of the man, as sold by Dunhill's Motorities.

STEERING-LINKED HEADLIGHTS

Luxury cars are usually among the first to sport the latest in technical innovations, and these often filter down to the more mundane machinery in due course only if the gadgets are felt to be a success and/or are financially viable.

One of the features available on Cadillac's fabulous V16, launched in 1930, was the option to have headlights that tracked with the steering, effectively allowing the driver to see around corners. Although simple to build, the idea was not widely taken up by other manufacturers, and the closest the idea got to the mass-market was when it appeared on the iconic and highly idiosyncratic Citroën DS of the 1960s and 1970s.

STEPNEY WHEEL

In the puncture-prone days of Edwardian motoring, a lot of effort and inventive thinking went into trying to alleviate the problem of deflation brought about by poor tyre construction and the copious amounts of horse-shoe nails littering the gravel roads.

Alongside charlatan claims from some manufacturers for puncture-proof tyres, a more measured approach to the problems of tyre changing came in the shape of the Stepney wheel, where the rim itself detached from the main body of the wheel. A replacement Stepney wheel with a good tyre would then be rapidly installed and the journey could resume once more with less hassle than in many other methods of puncture repair.

SWASTIKA – THE LUCKY MASCOT

Once upon a time, before the advent of Adolf Hitler and his poisonous doctrine, the swastika had an altogether more wholesome image, and was widely seen as a lucky symbol, rather like horseshoes. Its origins go back many centuries, and its rotation, either clockwise or anti-clockwise is of no great significance. The mound builders and cliff dwellers of Mexico, for instance, consider it a charm to drive away evil (somewhat ironically, considering its later usage) and bring good luck, long life and prosperity to the possessor.

Prior to the 1930s, the swastika was thus an emblem many people felt very comfortable with, and a number of manufacturers offered swastika mascots, such as this 1914 example, for fixing to the front of their cars.

Swastika.
The Lucky Mascot.

TALKING DASHBOARD

Seen as a Darwinian progression, the evolution of the car as a species has inevitably produced a number of cul-de-sacs. One such dead-end was the talking dashboard as fitted to early examples of the little-loved Austin Maestro. Launched in March 1983, it came with a number of advanced features including a bonded, laminated windscreen, a solid-state all electronic dashboard display, a trip computer, and the famed 'voice-synthesis warning and information system'.

This startling piece of technology was very much leading edge, and excited considerable interest from the press. Using the voice of Nicolette Mackenzie and just 32 words in its vocabulary (available in no less than 15 languages), it was unable to tell jokes or otherwise amuse its master, offering instead advice on low fuel levels, doors not properly shut or the need to wear seatbelts.

Living with it, however, rapidly grew tiresome, especially as the early cars suffered a veritable plague of electrical grmlins that resulted in Nicolette becoming something of an unwelcome chatterbox, and most owners soon reached for the off-switch.

TEFLON-COATED UMBRELLA

Whilst marketing people would have you believe it never rains, in the real world, we all know differently. So when the designers of the 2003 Rolls-Royce Phantom were busy redefining perfection, they took this into consideration.

In the leading edge of the rear doors, an umbrella was thoughtfully placed on each side, which could be deftly deployed by a chauffeur opening the door for his passenger. With typical thoroughness, however, Rolls-Royce's designers went the extra mile, covering the outside of the umbrella fabric in Teflon, which allowed it to be put back again still wet, without any risk of it subsequently rotting, ready for the next time.

TELETOUCH TRANSMISSION

As car designers looked towards the 1960s, their imaginations ran wild, often inventing solutions to problems that never really existed. One such example was the Teletouch transmission, as fitted in late 1957 to the spectacularly unloved Ford Edsel. This option did away with the need for a lever to engage the automatic gears, replacing it with buttons in the centre boss of the steering wheel.

This might have sounded like a pretty smart idea when on the drawing board, but once translated into the reality of driving on real roads, fatal flaws in the logic rapidly surfaced. Potential owners accustomed to finding a horn in centre of the steering wheel (especially in emergency situations) worried about the possibilities of confusion and mechanical meltdown if they instinctively hit the steering wheel centre in a moment of panic, throwing the car into reverse, park or neutral, or worse still, all three at once. In reality, this was impossible, but the public were not convinced, and labelled the system a distracting gimmick.

It was dropped as an option from the 1959 range of cars.

THERMADOR SWAMP COOLER

This bizarre-looking object from the 1950s was a cheap means of providing cooling to the interior of American cars in the days before air-conditioning was widely available. Fixed to the outside of the car window, it would funnel air through dampened pads, moistened by water, and from there, into the car. Obviously, relying on the cooling effect of water has its limitations, but in dry states such as Arizona and Texas, it was remarkably effective and could reduce the temperature of the car's interior from an unpleasant 100° F to a far more comfortable 70° F.

Today, they are highly collectible, and are seen as the must have for owners of 1950s American cars, looking for that final authentic touch.

THREE-POINT SAFETY BELT

Knowing their unique record for safety-related innovation, one should not be surprised that the Swedish firm of Volvo invented, and still holds the worldwide patent for the three-point safety belt (although no licence fee is ever charged for use by other manufacturers), or as it's more popularly know, the seat belt.

Its design was the work of Nils Bohlin, an aircraft engineer head-hunted by Volvo in 1958, and employed specifically to improve safety for car occupants. His design was refined from the analysis of many hundreds of hours of experimentation, and its simple design belies the effort that went into its conception. The seat belt, first fitted as standard by Volvo in 1959, is a fantastic piece of design, not only because of the countless lives saved by it, but because it is a model of simplicity to use, which further encourages people to use it.

TIGER TAIL

Following the slow resumption of motoring in the UK after the Second World War, many petrol companies wanted to build distinctive brands with which the public could identify, and on which they could build loyalty. The guys in marketing at Esso hit upon using a tiger as a powerful trademark, and successive marketing campaigns have featured the glorious animal in a number of different ways to achieve the company's objectives.

One such campaign came with the slogan 'Put a Tiger in your tank', and to help promote this idea, imitation tiger tails were sold, which drivers hung from their vehicle's petrol caps. Astonishingly, some 2,500,000 tiger tails were sold by the company over many years. Subsequent campaigns have featured expensively filmed tigers, but the tiger tail campaign is forever remembered as a part of the motoring scene of the late 1950s and 1960s.

TRAFFICATOR LIGHT SET

It's often said that experience is a hard taskmistress, and in the case of automotive inventiveness, these would appear to be well chosen words.

The Trafficator Light Set is a good example of just such a proof, in that it would appear to be a good idea to want to communicate your intentions to other road users before darting right across oncoming traffic. But fitting a set of three lights of different colours to each side of the car, in the blind faith that people will understand what your intentions are from a particular pattern of colours and be able to adjust their own course to accommodate this communication is perhaps at best optimistic. Perhaps predictably, the idea did not catch on.

VASE

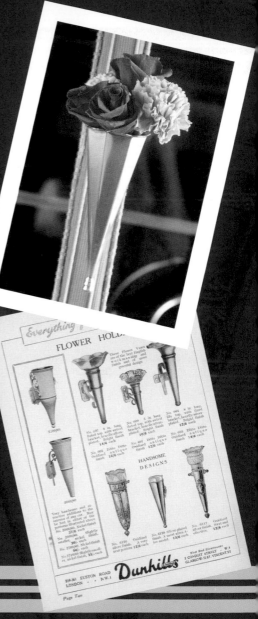

Owners of early enclosed cars were invariably hugely wealthy individuals who liked their luxuries, and saw no merit in restraint. The interiors of their cars rather predictably proved an almost irresistible canvas on which to reflect this love of the finer things.

Among the superb fittings an owner could specify were a speaking-tube with which to give orders to the chauffeur, parallel cords in the headlining for holding a passenger's top-hat, and even a beautiful cut-glass vase for holding a fresh flower and giving the final touch to this coach-built comfort-zone. Such vases were offered in a number of Edwardian motorist catalogues, including Brown Brothers and Dunhill's Motorities, should your car not come fitted with one as standard.

VOLVO PETROL CAN

Whilst in some countries the carrying of a spare can of petrol is now illegal, many owners, particularly of older cars whose gauges have long since stopped telling anything resembling the truth, always carry a spare gallon or two. With petrol being the inherently dangerous substance it is, those countries still prepared to allow their motorists this safety net have laws regarding what container it should or should not be carried in.

It takes the clear thinking of the Swedes, however, to look at a problem and come up with a truly sensible solution to the problem of how to stop the can sliding unhindered around the boot: make it to fit snugly inside the spare wheel. Holding six litres, this fantastically simple solution has not been available, unfortunately, for many years.

WASHING BOOTS

Cleaning the car has always been a messy affair, but in the early days, when absolutely everything had to be washed thoroughly, corners could not be cut. These cars had fittings made from brass, copper, nickel etc, whilst there was also a high wood content that could not be allowed to stay dirty if the car was to remain in good condition.

With most roads, especially anything outside the cities, still little better than gravel tracks, cars got messy quickly, and needed regular and thorough washing. Obviously, the wealthy owner would not wash it himself, but being the caring type, would no doubt be keen to ensure that the cleaner was properly attired for the job, and for many years, catalogues such as Dunhill's Motorities offered the washing boots pictured.

With such boots, function clearly mattered more than form, and whilst to modern eyes, they may look not entirely unlike the sort of footwear Frankenstein's monster might have worn, they were most definitely suited to the task.

3242
RUBBER WASHING BOOT,
with thigh extension. .. **32/6**

WATER-REPELLENT GLASS

The invention and subsequent adoption of windscreen wipers was an obvious step in the right direction for motoring safety. However, whilst for the vast majority of the time, drivers look through the forward-facing pane of glass, there are occasions during a journey on a wet day when it could be argued that safety is compromised by wet side windows.

For just such moments, the safety-obsessed boffins at Volvo who have slaved tirelessly for decades to improve the lot of motorists in accidents, researched and subsequently specified the fitting of WRG (water-repellent glass) to the front side windows of their cars from 2004 onwards. This laminated glass has a hydrophobic surface with high water-sliding properties that gathers together the droplets of water which are then blown away, leaving the glass clean and dry, and ultimately, that little bit safer.

WINDSCREEN WIPER KIT

The concept of a car without windscreen wipers is almost unimaginable to anyone born since the resumption of motoring in 1945. Whilst most of us have been in cars where the wipers' efficiency has been patchy, the thought of being caught in rain without the ability to see the road ahead through a regularly cleared screen is beyond comprehension.

Yet, for most of the first four decades of the car's life, whilst rudimentary systems were available, their fitment was not mandatory. After-market kits such as this, on sale in the Brown Brothers' catalogue of 1933 offered great steps forward toward safer motoring, but such luxuries as variable speed and intermittent wipe were still a long way off.

LUCAS WINDSCREEN WIPERS.

LUCAS No. 30.
Suction Operated.
An improved model for 1933. It has a wider angle of wipe and is more powerful, which greatly facilitates operation on hills or under other full-throttle conditions.
Ebony Black.

No.   Each.
W5/50b/1408 ..   19/6
Nickel-plated.
W5/50/1509 ..   21/-
Dash Valve Control.
W5/51/100   1/3

LUCAS No. RW1.
Electric.
A new dual arm Wiper with motor and gear box as separate units. Wiper arms are fitted with 9-in. twin rubber blades, each giving 160° angle of wipe. Motor is self-starting and wiper starts as soon as switch is operated. Ebony Black and Chromium. Complete with separate switch.   ..   each 72/6

No. W5/93/5405

LUCAS No. CW.
Electric.
A new model for 1933 with several new features. Motor is self-starting, i.e., Wiper starts immediately switch is "on." A "parking" position is provided which locks switch in the "off" position and wiper arm out of line of vision. Interchangeable with old MT types. Ebony Black only.

LUCAS TYPE CW1

Single Arm.
No. W5/94/1902
Each 25/6

Dual Arm.
No. W5/95/2700
Each 36/-